Math Smarts

Tips, Tricks, and Secrets for Making Math More Fun!

By Lynette Long, Ph.D.
Illustrated by Tracy McGuinness

★ AmericanGirl™

Published by Pleasant Company Publications

Questions or comments? Call 1-800-845-0005, visit our Web site
at **americangirl.com,** or write Customer Service, American Girl,
8400 Fairway Place, Middleton, WI 53562-0497.

Printed in China
06 07 08 09 10 C&C 12 11 10 9 8 7

Editorial Development: Sara Hunt, Michelle Watkins

Art Direction and Design: Camela Decaire

Production: Kendra Pulvermacher, Mindy Rappe, Jeannette Bailey, Judith Lary

Photography: Jamie Young, Sandy May

Library of Congress Cataloging-in-Publication Data

Long, Lynette

Math smarts : tips for learning, using and remembering math! / by Lynette
Long ; illustrated by Tracy McGuinness.

p. cm.

"American Girl Library"

Summary: Describes the importance of mathematics in everyday life and offers
advice on how to make learning math skills easier.

ISBN 1-58485-875-3 (pbk.)

i. Arithmetic—Juvenile literature. [1. Arithmetic.] I. McGuinness, Tracy. ill
II. American girl (Middleton, Wis.) III. Title.

QA135.6.L68 2004   513_dc22   2003060909

Dear Reader,

Whether you want to improve your understanding
of math concepts that you learn in school,
or you want to see how math will help you
in the real world, you'll find fun, useful
tips and tricks in this book. Plus, you'll find a
handy multiplication and division Smart Chart at
the back of the book to take with you wherever
you go!

One of the coolest things about math is that
every problem has an answer. And, although it's
sometimes challenging to find that one right
answer, when you do, it feels great!

Explore *Math Smarts* and have some fun with math.
You're your own guide-no teachers, no timed
tests, and, best of all, no grades!

Your friends at American Girl

Contents

MATH FUN 33

Multiplication practice &
division rules

TESTING, TESTING 47

Test-taking tips to help
you score

MATH IS EVERYWHERE 53

Learn about math in the real world—
even fill out a check!

Date:..............................

1246

Pay to the
Order of ....
.... Dollars

$

THE HAPPY
PIGGY BANK

Memo ....

035001577 XX 00652618745 XX 1246

Date:..............................

1247

$

Dollars

00652618745 XX 1247

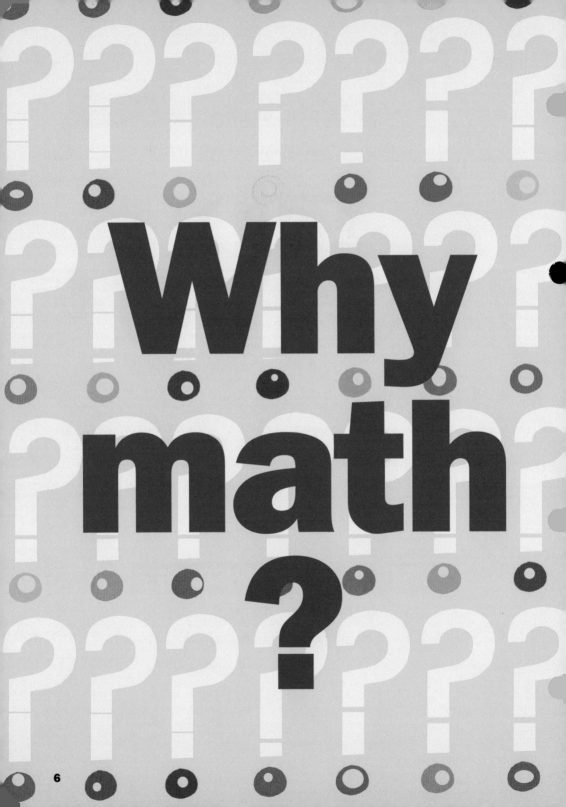

Why math?

Because . . .

Math Matters NOW!

Think about how your math skills can help you every day and you'll see just how important knowing math really is!

If you can do math, you can:

Double a recipe when baking holiday cookies for your friends

Make sure you get the right change when you buy earrings at the mall

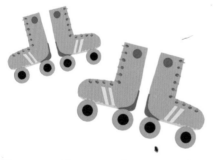

Figure out how much you need to save each week to buy new Rollerblades

Determine how long you'll need to stay busy in the car on your summer trip

Estimate how much paint to buy when you're painting your bedroom

Figure out how much fabric you need to make curtains or pillows for your room

Equally divvy up a pizza among your sleepover guests

Help Dad figure out how much to tip the server at the restaurant

Determine how much you'll spend for a movie ticket plus a tub of popcorn and a soda

Figure out the price of that cool shirt on the 25-percent-off rack

Calculate how much you would get paid for a babysitting job

Help plan the school dance on budget

Set prices for your crafts at the school fair so that you actually make money

Calculate the cost of a mini Eiffel Tower souvenir when you travel to Paris

Math Matters LATER!

Picture yourself when you get older. What do you think you'll do? Do you think your job will require you to know math? On the list below, check off which careers you think require good math skills.

Accountant	Flight attendant	Pharmacist
Advertising executive	Fundraiser	Photographer
Aerospace engineer	Golf pro	Piano repairperson
Astronaut	Graphic designer	Pilot
Athlete	Hair stylist	Police officer
Chef	House painter	Real estate agent
Computer analyst	Insurance agent	Roller coaster designer
Dentist	Interior designer	Salesclerk
Doctor	Lawyer	Schoolteacher
Editor	Lifeguard	Scientist
Electrical engineer	Loan officer	Shop owner
Entertainer	Market analyst	Sportscaster
Farmer	Mom	Travel agent
Fashion designer	Musician	Veterinarian
Film producer	Newspaper reporter	Video game designer
Firefighter	Nurse	Wedding planner

Answer: All of them! No matter what you do when you grow up, skills in math will help you every day.

Math at Work

So, you want to be a veterinarian? You get to make pet owners happy by helping their injured or sick animals. AND you get to put all those math skills to good use!

That's right! Vets use math when they:

- Calculate doses of medicine. A dose is based on the weight of the animal.

- Compute an animal's heart rate, blood pressure, and respiration rate

- Run the business side of their practices, too—setting fees, paying bills, and preparing invoices

BIG
Truth

Math will be part of your life
today and tomorrow.

It's never too late
to do better at math.

Attitude Check

It's All About Attitude

Read each of the following statements, then check whether it applies to you or your feelings about math.

Me   Not me

1. I answer questions in math class.

2. I don't feel nervous before math tests.

3. I do my math homework first.

4. Math is interesting to me.

5. I enjoy working with numbers.

6. I feel smart in math class.

7. I think math is fun.

Total

If you answered "Not me" to three or more of the questions, your thoughts may be making you nervous. Try not to psych yourself out. Even if you checked just one or two (or none!), new ways of thinking about math might come in handy sometime in your future. Check out the ideas on the next page!

Do you need a new mathi'tude?

Change your thoughts, and your attitude will change, too!

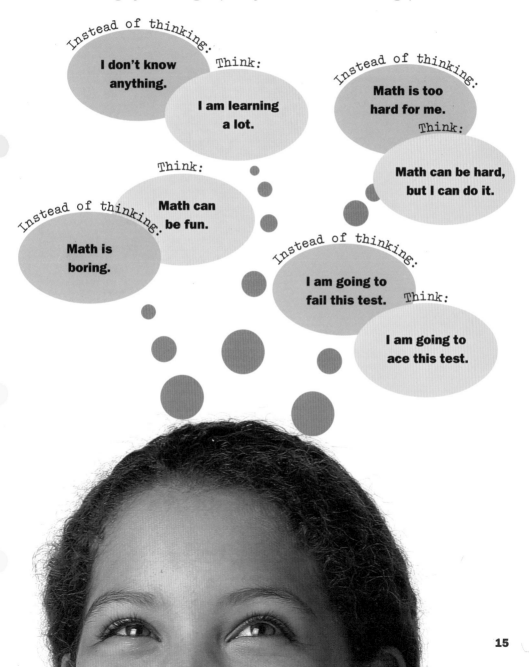

Math
Learning Ladder

trigonometry

geometry

algebra

percentages

decimals

Unlike some other classes you will take, *everything* you learn in math builds on what you learned before. You really need to understand each math concept before you move on to the next level.

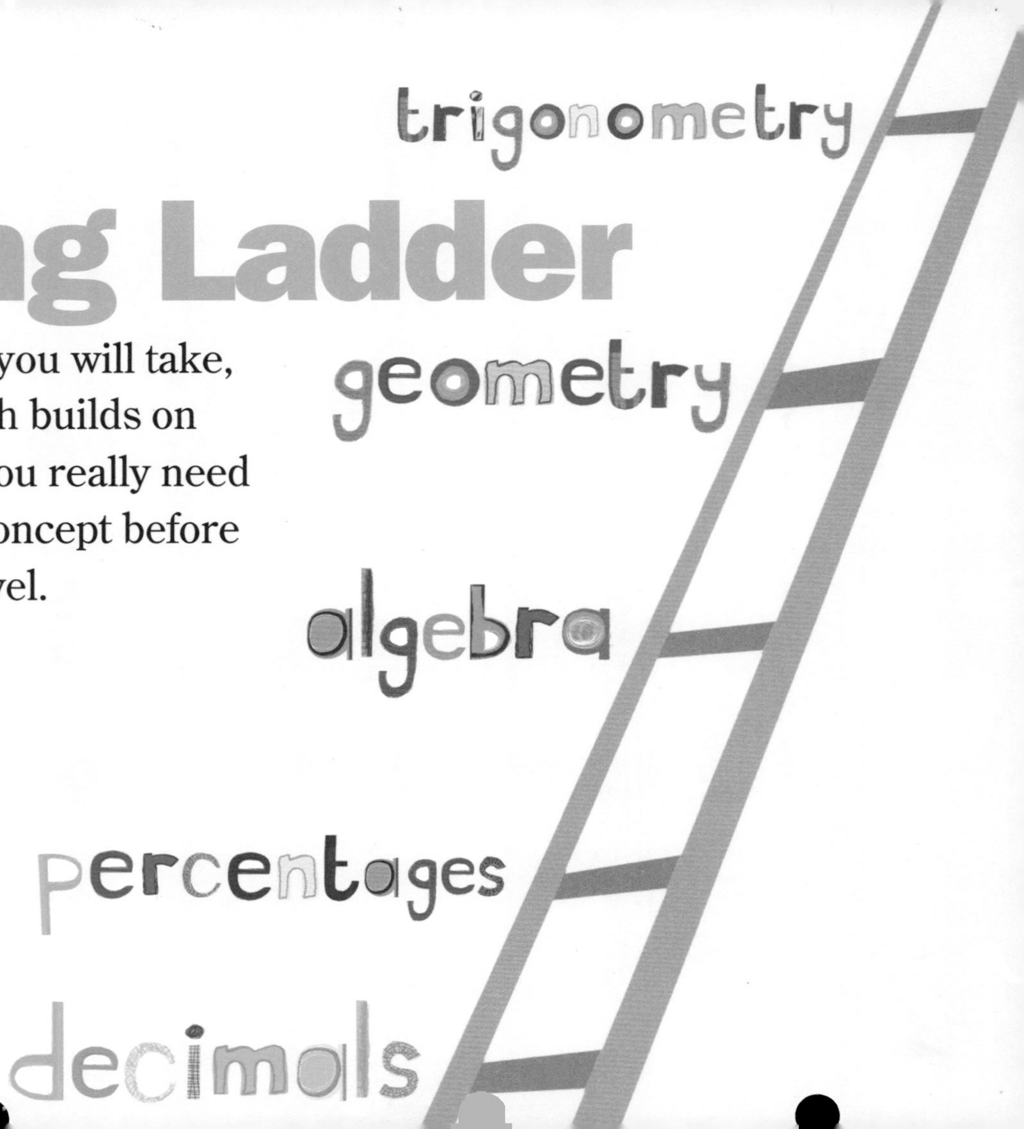

Don't Give Up!

If you're having trouble with math, look closely at what you've learned so far. It may be that all you need to do is back up and make sure you have the previous steps down pat. Sometimes you need to step back before you can move up!

fractions

division

multiplication

addition and subtraction

BIG Truth.

Attitude counts.
A good attitude multiplies.

Get
Going

How Do You Learn Best?

What are the best ways for you to study math? There are seven different types of study smarts. Learning what kind of smarts you have can help you study. Check all of the statements that apply to you.

☑ I like to sing.　　　☑ I work better by myself.

☑ I like to make things with my hands.　☑ I am athletic.

☑ I am a good writer.　☑ Other people really like me.

☐ I can carry a tune.　☐ I am good at jigsaw puzzles.

☑ I have excellent people skills.　☑ I like to draw.

(Love to)

☐ I enjoy playing word games.　☑ Numbers are easy for me.

☑ I like to play strategy games like checkers and chess.

☑ I can feel the beat of music.　☑ I am a leader.

☑ I enjoy reading.　☐ I can control my emotions.

☑ Mazes are easy for me to do.　☑ I play an instrument.

☑ I like to touch things when I learn.

☑ I understand the differences between similar words.

☑ I enjoy science experiments. ☑ I am very active. *Yesss!!!*

☑ I learn best when I am moving. ☑ I can motivate myself.

☑ I can find my way anywhere (without getting lost)! *maybe*

☑ I like solving math puzzles. ☑ I am really organized.

☑ I know my strengths and my weaknesses.

things to do
1.
2.
3.
4.
5.

☑ I remember song lyrics after hearing them a few times.

☑ I am a good communicator. ☑ I ~~think~~ *know* I am creative.

☑ I am intrigued by mysteries. ☑ I like to spend time alone.

☑ I love to be with friends.

Count how many boxes of each color you checked. Then turn the page to see how your smarts can help you study.

3	3	4	4	2	3	5
red	**purple**	**blue**	**violet**	**aqua**	**green**	**orange**

Put Your Smarts to Work for You!

If you checked mostly **red,** you have **self smarts.** Try studying on your own. Reward yourself by calling a friend on the phone, watching TV, or listening to music after you finish a certain amount of work.

If you checked mostly **purple,** you have **musical smarts.** Study by singing your math formulas. Make up songs about your math notes or multiplication tables.

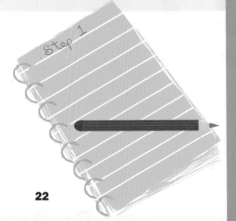

If you checked mostly **blue,** you have **physical smarts.** Use household objects to work out your math problems. Or recite your multiplication tables while jumping rope.

If you checked mostly **violet,** you have **logical smarts.** Try breaking down math problems into numbered steps. Learn the steps in order, and you'll remember how to do any problem.

If you checked mostly **aqua,** you have **spatial smarts.** Draw pictures of the math problems.

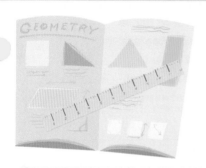

If you checked mostly **green,** you have **language smarts.** Take notes from your textbook, translating what's in the book into your own words. Use rhymes to remember math facts.

If you checked mostly **orange,** you have **people smarts.** Form a study group with friends, or have someone else quiz you.

You might have a little bit of many types of smarts. Try any of these ideas (regardless of how you scored) to find out what works best for you.

Math Stuff

Keep all of your math supplies in one place. Then, when it's time to do your homework, you'll have what you need right at your fingertips.

Make sure you have a ruler, compass, and protractor at home, too, if you're using these tools at school. Then you don't have to worry about carrying everything back and forth. You're always prepared.

markers

highlighter

colored pencils

ruler

protractor

folder for old tests

graph paper

compass

pencil

A sharp pencil point makes you feel sharp.

pencil sharpener

eraser

Keeps your papers neat and helps keep you (and your teacher!) from getting confused

calculator

paper

Take Note!

Make the most of your time in math class. Taking good notes in class will help you with homework *and* when it's time to study for a test. Here are some neat note-taking tips.

1. Date your notes.

2. Math is like a foreign language. There are lots of new words to learn. Underline the new words and write the definitions.

3. Highlight the math rules and formulas.

4. Use diagrams to illustrate the problem.

5. Copy down all examples. Label all the steps in the example.

October 5 **1.**

2. Simplifying fractions

to simplify a fraction, divide the numerator and denominator by the same number

3. a fraction is in its lowest terms when it can't be simplified any more

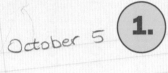 **4.**

1) numerator ⟶ $\dfrac{3}{12}$
   denominator ⟶
   ⟹ (down)

5. STEP 1: what # goes into both 3 and 12? 3

STEP 2: divide $\dfrac{3}{12}$ $(3 \div 3) = \dfrac{1}{4}$
                               $(12 \div 3) =$

★ ANSWER: $\dfrac{1}{4}$ ★

2) Simplify $\dfrac{6}{18}$

STEP 1: what # goes into 6 and 18? 3

STEP 2: divide $\dfrac{6}{18} = \dfrac{(6 \div 3)}{(18 \div 3)} = \dfrac{2}{6}$

simplify again (STEP 1). What # goes into 2 and 6? 2

$\dfrac{2}{6} = \dfrac{(2 \div 2)}{(6 \div 2)} = \dfrac{1}{3}$

⟶ LOWEST

27

Got a test?
Here are the
Top 10
Study Strategies

10. Take notes about what the teacher says is going to be on the test.

9. Don't wait until the last minute to study.

8. Start each study session by reviewing your notes.

7. Make flash cards for formulas you need to memorize.

6. If you have trouble with a certain type of problem, do extra problems of the same type.

5. Copy all the example problems in the chapter.

4. Correct and review all old tests and quizzes.

3. Find a study partner and teach her the information.

2. Take a practice test.

1. Reward yourself!
Make a list of things you like to do that take 10 minutes or less. When you're finished studying, do one of them!

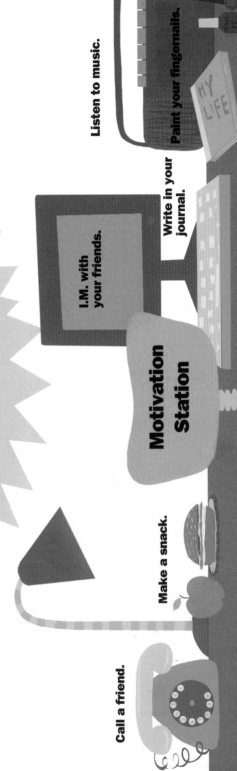

Motivation Station

I.M. with your friends.

Write in your journal.

Listen to music.

Paint your fingernails.

MY LIFE

Make a snack.

Call a friend.

Study Tips from Girls

Buy a blank cassette tape and record all your notes on the tape. Listen to your notes while you're getting dressed, in the shower, and before you go to bed. I'll bet you get a great grade on your next test.
Christine

I use flash cards to study for math tests. I write all the formulas on the cards and carry them with me wherever I go. It helps a lot. Try it.
Frannie

Always believe in yourself. Never think about the bad grade you might get on your math test. Remember *The Little Engine That Could*, the story that your parents read you when you were three years old: "I think I can, I think I can."
Casey

Try reading through your work every day at the end of the day, or even right after the class. Take it from me, it works like magic.
Dorothy

I make a list of everything I need to know. Then I check it off as I learn it.
Alberta

If you are working on a hard math problem at school, try writing the problem on sticky notes. Put them on the light switch and in the bathroom where you put your tooth-brush, and even on the phone. After a few days, you will probably learn it. It worked for me!
Katy

When I study for a math class, I study with my best friend, because she's good at math, too. We help each other by making up fake quizzes.
Kate

Here's a fun way to learn your math facts. All you need is sidewalk chalk and a flat driveway. First make a long path with the chalk on the driveway. Write math facts in some places on the path. Then go along the path hopscotch-style, and each time you get to a math fact, say the answer.
Maddie

Classical music does the trick for me! Turn on some classical music and read over your math stuff to study. You will remember it like it was just told to you!
Kitty

31

BIG
Truth

Math is like a sport.
You have to practice.

The key is to make practicing fun.

Math
Fun

Tricks and Tips

Try some of these tips to jump-start your memory.

When Multiplying by . . .

0 The answer is always zero. Zip. Zilch. Nada.
7 x 0 = 0

1 The answer is always the number you are multiplying.
7 x 1 = 7

2 Just double the number, or add the number to itself!
7 x 2 = 14, or 7 + 7 = 14

3 Double the number, then add one more of it.
7 x 3 = 21, or 7 + 7 = 14, and 14 + 7 = 21

4 You use a double-double—double the number, then double the answer.
7 x 4 = 28, or 7 + 7 = 14, and 14 + 14 = 28

5 Count by 5s—OR multiply by 10 and divide the answer in half.
7 x 5 = 35, or 7 x 10 = 70 and 70 ÷ 2 = 35

7 Use two answers easier to find: Times 5 plus times 2.
7 x 7 = 49, or 7 x 5 = 35 and 7 x 2 = 14, and 35 + 14 = 49

9 Take a shortcut. Multiply by 10, then subtract one of the multiple.
7 x 9 = 63, or 7 x 10 = 70 and 70 − 7 = 63

10 Just add a zero.
7 x 10 = 70

Rhyme Time

For certain multiplication facts, you can make up rhymes to help you. Try these rhymes to help with your *times*.

Eight and eight fell on the floor.
When they got up, they were 64.

Seven and eight picked up sticks.
They found a total of 56.

Six and eight were very late.
The number of minutes was 48.

Five, six, seven, eight.
Fifty-six is seven times eight.

Five and five jump and dive.
Five times five is 25.

One, two, three, four.
One-two is three times four.

Reverse It

If you don't know a fact, reverse it. Do you know the answer now? What's 7 x 3? Don't know? Try 3 x 7. Know it now?

Quick Change

Use coins to illustrate a problem you're trying to solve.
If the problem is 9 x 3, make 9 piles of 3 pennies. Counting by threes, can you figure it out? To double-check, combine all the pennies and count how many.

Multiplication

To master those multiplication facts, find fun new ways to practice, practice, practice.

Kooky Cookie Game

Draw a big tic-tac-toe board. Two players each get a different kind of cookie to play (chocolate and vanilla sandwich cookies work well!). Both players roll a single die at the same time and multiply the two numbers on the dice. Whoever shouts the right answer first puts a cookie on the tic-tac-toe board. The first to get three cookies in a row wins!

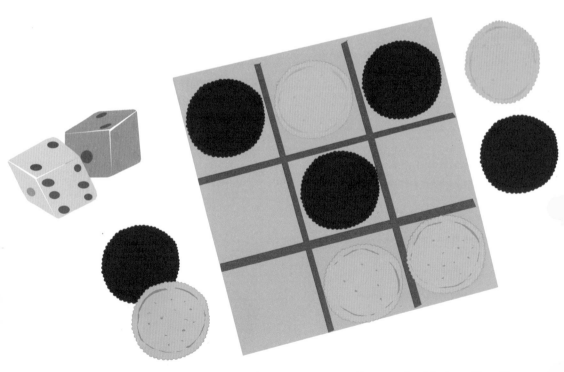

Challenge: Each player rolls 2 dice at the same time and adds together the numbers on both sets of dice. Then each player multiplies the two totals (same as before). The first player to shout the right answer puts a cookie on the tic-tac-toe board. The first to get three cookies in a row wins.

Practice

Address 4 Fun

On your next family road trip, pick a building or house you pass and multiply the numbers in the address. For example, 1325 Alpine Circle would be 1 x 3 x 2 x 5 = 30, and 7913 Maple Avenue would be 7 x 9 x 1 x 3 = 189.

Have everyone join in the fun and see who gets the largest product. Be careful: bigger street numbers don't always net the biggest answers!

Times to Go

You can practice with your flash cards by quizzing someone else. Keep a set in the backseat, then call out the problems and test your mom as she drives you to soccer practice.

Sound Off

Get everyone involved. Have all the passengers count off by 2s, 4s, 6s, or 8s. Then pick up the speed and see who goofs first!

Psst!

Division is just multiplication backward.

Don't know what 54 divided by 9 is?

Change $54 \div 9$ into

$$? \times 9 = 54$$

$$6$$

That's the answer to your division problem.

$$54 \div 9 = 6$$

Division Rules

1. Every number is divisible by 1.

2. Every even number is divisible by 2.

3. If the sum of the digits of a number is divisible by 3, the number is divisible by 3.

4. If the last two digits are divisible by 4, the number is divisible by 4.

5. If a number ends in 0 or 5, it is divisible by 5.

6. If a number is divisible by 2 and 3, it is divisible by 6.

7. The only way to tell if a number is divisible by 7 is to try it!

8. If the last three digits of a number are divisible by 8, the number is divisible by 8.

9. If the sum of the digits of a number equals 9, the number is divisible by 9.

10. If the number ends in 0, it is divisible by 10.

Prime Time

News flash: When you solve this puzzle, you find the numbers that are prime.

Prime numbers are numbers that are divisible only by themselves and one. For example, 7 is divisible only by 7 and 1, so 7 is a prime number. To figure out all the prime numbers from 1 to 100, first put a triangle around the number 1, since 1 is not a prime number and it is not a multiple. Put a circle around the number 2, the first prime number, and then cross out all the multiples of 2. Now put a circle around the next prime number, 3, and cross out all the multiples of 3. Keep going, starting back at the top each time, until all the remaining numbers are either crossed out or circled.

Make a list of the prime numbers you found.

....

....

....

1	2	3	4	5	6	7	8	9	10
11	12	13	14	15	16	17	18	19	20
21	22	23	24	25	26	27	28	29	30
31	32	33	34	35	36	37	38	39	40
41	42	43	44	45	46	47	48	49	50
51	52	53	54	55	56	57	58	59	60
61	62	63	64	65	66	67	68	69	70
71	72	73	74	75	76	77	78	79	80
81	82	83	84	85	86	87	88	89	90
91	92	93	94	95	96	97	98	99	100

Answers: 2, 3, 5, 7, 11, 13, 17, 19, 23, 29, 31, 37, 41, 43, 47, 53, 59, 61, 67, 71, 73, 79, 83, 89, 97

Just the Factors Game

Play this game with your friends—you'll barely realize that you're practicing your division facts!

START → **7** **10** **9**

8 **33** **16**

2 **4** **2o**

You will need: 2 game markers (for example, use coins, buttons, or pebbles) and 1 die. Put the 2 markers on the start space. Roll the die and move your piece the number of spaces on the die. If the number on the new space can be divided (is divisible) by the number on the die, you may keep your piece there. If the number on the new space is not evenly divisible by the number on the die, move your piece back to its original space. The first person to get to the finish spot wins.

12

15

25

30

FINISH

21

6

18

24

Word Problems

Think of word problems as mysteries that you need to solve. Carefully keep track of the facts you know to figure out the answer.

Trick 1
Act It Out

Make the word problem come alive using objects in your home. Here's an example:

Problem: **If Jane is 2 years older than Emily, and Sarah is 5 years younger than Jane, how old is Emily, if Sarah is 7?**

Strategy: **Use three stuffed animals to act out the problem. Give each animal the name of one of the characters in the story. Move your animals around and put them from oldest to youngest. Now figure out how old Emily is.**

Trick 2
Trial and Error

Problem: The students at Central Middle School sold 200 tickets for an 8 p.m. cheerleading competition. Adult tickets were $5 each. Children's tickets were $2 each. If a total of $850 was collected, how many adult tickets and children's tickets were sold?

Strategy: To get your answer, you'll need to pick 2 numbers that add up to 200. It's a good idea to start in the middle—with 100 adult tickets and 100 children's tickets—to get an idea of which direction you need to go to get your answer.

$$\begin{array}{r} 100 \\ \times\ 5 \\ \hline \end{array} \qquad \begin{array}{r} 100 \\ \times\ 2 \\ \hline \end{array} \qquad \begin{array}{r} 500 \\ +\ 200 \\ \hline \end{array}$$

$$\$500 \quad \$200 \quad \$700$$

Since this is less than $850, you will need more adult tickets. Try 125 adult tickets and 75 children's tickets.

$$\begin{array}{r} 125 \\ \times\ 5 \\ \hline \end{array} \qquad \begin{array}{r} 75 \\ \times\ 2 \\ \hline \end{array} \qquad \begin{array}{r} 625 \\ +\ 150 \\ \hline \end{array}$$

$$\$625 \quad \$150 \quad \$775$$

Closer. Now try 150 adult and 50 children's tickets. What happens?

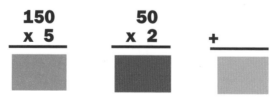

$$\begin{array}{r} 150 \\ \times\ 5 \\ \hline \end{array} \qquad \begin{array}{r} 50 \\ \times\ 2 \\ \hline \end{array} \qquad +\ \underline{}$$

BIG
Truth

**Math is all about patterns.
When you find the patterns,
you'll see math in a whole new way.**

Testing, Testing

FRESHLY BAKED

A Dozen Test-Taking Tips

Circle or put a box around each answer so that your teacher can spot it.

If you need extra time, politely ask for it. The worst your teacher can say is no.

Double-check your answers. It's easy to make a careless mistake.

Show your work. Most teachers will give you credit for your work even if your answer is wrong.

Skip difficult problems. Don't waste time on problems you don't understand.

Look at your answers and see if they make sense. If they don't seem right, they probably aren't.

Ask the teacher for help if you don't understand the directions.

Show the units for your answers. Put inches, feet, meters after the answer.

Write your name on your paper. Read all the directions carefully.

Reduce all fractions to the lowest terms.

As soon as you get your test, write down all the formulas or important facts you've memorized.

A test is not a race. The person who hands in her test first usually does NOT get the highest grade. Take your time.

THE DONUT SHOP

When you get your test back . . .

Do:

- Save it to study for future tests
- Correct all the answers you got wrong
- Make sure you understand how to do the problems you got wrong
- Get help if you need it

Don't:

- Throw it in the trash
- Lie to your parents about your grade
- Brag to students who scored lower than you

Test Strategies

Go into your math tests with these simple strategies. You might come out with better grades.

Multiple Choice Questions

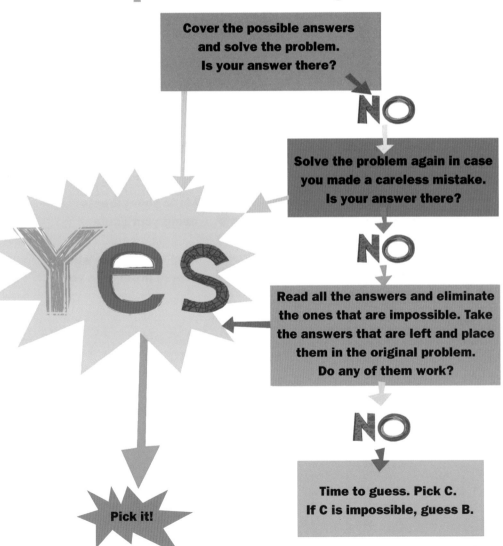

Cover the possible answers and solve the problem. Is your answer there?

NO

Solve the problem again in case you made a careless mistake. Is your answer there?

NO

Read all the answers and eliminate the ones that are impossible. Take the answers that are left and place them in the original problem. Do any of them work?

NO

Yes

Pick it!

Time to guess. Pick C. If C is impossible, guess B.

True-False Questions

Question
Circles are always bigger than squares.

Answer
FALSE
Circles are sometimes bigger than squares.

Trick
Whenever you see the word "always" in a true-false problem, the answer is usually false.

Question
6 x 4 = 24

Answer
TRUE
6 x 4 is 24.

Trick
None!

Question
6 x 3 = 18 and 7 x 3 = 24

Answer
FALSE

Trick
If the word "and" is in a true-false problem, both parts of the sentence must be true for the sentence to be true. Since 7 x 3 is not 24, the answer is false.

Help!

Q: I have been doing very badly on my math tests. My last score was a 58. I really try hard and I ask for help. I study, but I still get bad grades. My mom wants to get me a tutor, but I don't want that!

A: Your mom wants to get you a tutor because she **cares** about you and she wants you to **do well** in math. Tutors can be fun. They can teach you a lot of tricks and **explain things** you don't understand. Get a math tutor and work with her, and your scores will surely go up.

Q: I do pretty well in school. But I'm not doing as well as I know I can. I want someone to help me in my math class, but I don't want my friends to know. My mom sees that my grades are slipping. I would get a tutor, but my life is so busy. Help!

A: Admitting that you can do better is the first step. Now, if you can only find time for that tutor. **Look** at your schedule and **set some priorities.** Math will be useful over and over as you get older. Do the other activities that are taking your time count as much?

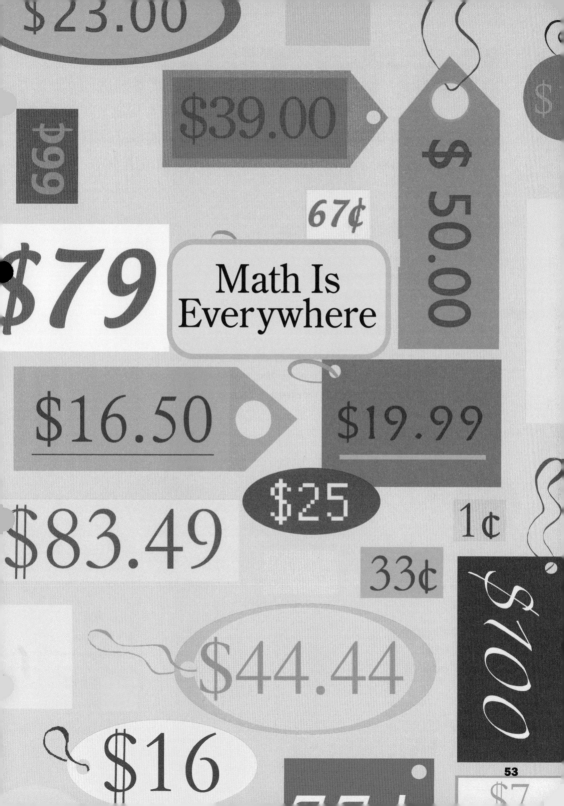

$23.00

66¢

$39.00

$50.00

$

67¢

$79

Math Is
Everywhere

$16.50

$19.99

$25

1¢

$83.49

33¢

$100

$44.44

$16

$7

53

Party Time

Figuring fractions and equivalents are just a few ways you'll use math to stir up some punch for your friends.

Rainbow Punch

You will need:
- ½ gallon rainbow sherbet
- 10 cups cold ginger ale
  (approximately one 2-liter bottle, plus 2 cups)
- maraschino cherries (optional)

When it's party time, scoop sherbet into the punch bowl. Slowly pour the cold ginger ale over the sherbet, and stir carefully. Serve right away. If desired, place a cherry in each cup. Makes 4½ quarts.

Standard Equivalents

16 tablespoons
= 1 cup
= 8 ounces

2 cups
= 1 pint
= 16 ounces

2 pints
= 1 quart
= 32 ounces

4 quarts
= 1 gallon
= 128 ounces

If you are having 12 friends over, will you have enough punch for everyone to have 2 cups? Your punch cups hold 4 ounces (oz.) each.

How much does it make?

quarts = [ ] oz.

How much do you need?

[ ] x [ ] = [ ] cups

(friends)   (cups)

[ ] cups x [ ] oz. = [ ] oz.

So, will you have enough for everyone to have 2 cups?_____

Can you figure out how to make a half batch of punch?

[ ] pints rainbow sherbet

[ ] cups ginger ale

makes [ ] oz. or [ ] 4-oz. cups

In Your Room

You want to paint your walls Blue Kazoo. How much paint do you need—one can or two?

How Many Cans?

1. Use a tape measure to measure the wall height in feet (for example, 96 inches = 8 feet).

2. Measure the width of each wall to be painted in feet. (If your measurement is in inches, divide by 12 and round up to the nearest whole number.)

3. Add all width measurements together.

4. Multiply the height (Step 1) by the total width (Step 3) to get the total square footage of wall space.

5. Measure the height and width of each window in feet. Multiply the height by the width to figure out the unpainted area for each window.

6. Repeat Step 5 for any doors.

7. Total the unpainted area.

8. Subtract the total in Step 7 from the total in Step 4 to determine the total wall area to be painted.

9. Divide the total in Step 8 by the coverage rate listed on the paint can. (The coverage rate for Blue Kazoo is 350 square feet per gallon.)

   Remember: You'll need twice as much for two coats of paint.

1. Wall height [ ]

2. Wall width [ ] **+** [ ] **+** [ ] **+**

3. Total wall width [ ]

4. Total wall area
(height x width)...

Step 1 [ ] **✗** Step 3 [ ] square feet [ ]

5. Window area
	height		width		square feet
Window 1	[ ]	✗	[ ]	=	[ ]
					+
Window 2	[ ]	✗	[ ]	=	[ ]

6. Door area
					+
Door 1	[ ]	✗	[ ]	=	[ ]
					+
Door 2	[ ]	✗	[ ]	=	[ ]

7. Total unpainted square footage
(windows and doors) .... [ ]

8. Total
wall area   Step 4 [ ] **–** Unpainted
wall area   Step 7 [ ] **=** [ ]

9. Painted
area   Step 8 [ ] **÷** Square
feet/gallon   Coverage rate [ ] **=** [ ]

can(s) per coat
(round up to the
nearest whole number)

57

Sale Seeker

You'll be a smarter shopper when you bring your math skills with you to the mall.

Common Percents

You find the fuzzy sweater that you've had your eye on in the color you like . . . and it's on sale! If it costs $30.00 regularly, and is marked 25 percent (%) off, do you know how much it costs?

A simple way to calculate 25% is to first figure out 10% (by dropping the last digit and moving the decimal point one place to the left).

Regular price

10% (drop last digit and move the decimal point) +

10% (again) +

5% (half of 10%)

—————————————

Total discount

Sale price (regular price – discount)

The next time you're at the mall, the sweater is 50% off the "already reduced" price—that's HALF the sale price.

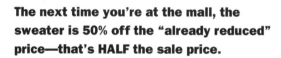

÷ 2 =

Sale price (50%) **Clearance price**

If your allowance is $5.00 per week, how long would it take you to save for the sweater? (Your piggy bank is empty.)

Weeks

Is it worth it? Only **you** can figure that out!

Check It Out!

Instead of carrying lots of cash, using a checking account gives you an easier way to pay.

A check is a piece of paper that lets you spend money from your checking account. When you write a check, the check is sent to your bank. The dollar amount on the check is withdrawn from your account and sent to the person to whom you wrote the check. You can only write checks for up to the amount of money that you have in your account.

It's important to use your check register to keep track of every check you write and any withdrawals or deposits you make so that you always know the balance, or how much money you have, in your account.

Try this:

Pretend you have a checking account with a balance of $37.00. You wrote one check to Ellie's Deli for lunch for $7.50. Then you emptied your piggy bank and counted out $4.65 in change, which you deposited into your account. What's your current balance?

Check Register

Number	Date	Transaction	Payment (−)	Deposit (+)	Balance
		starting balance			37.00
1245	7/11	Ellie's Deli	7.50		
	7/13			4.65	

Write out the two checks below to make two (pretend) purchases for your mom's birthday celebration:

Faux Flower Shoppe $15.75
Costume Jeweler $10.40

Don't forget to sign your name, and remember to enter these checks in your register. What's your new balance? _____

Check number

1246

Date: ....

Write the name of the person or business you're paying here.

Fill in the dollar amount in numbers here.

$

Pay to the
Order of .... Dollars

Write out the amount of the check in words here.

Sign your name here.

THE HAPPY

$

PIGGY BANK

Memo ....

These numbers indicate your account number and the check number, as well as which bank you use.

035001577 XX 0065261Ô745 XX 1246

1247

Date: ....

Pay to the
Order of ....

$

.... Dollars

THE HAPPY

$

PIGGY BANK

Memo ....

035001577 XX 0065261Ô745 XX 1247

Answers: The balance after lunch and your deposit is $34.15, which leaves you with $8.00 after shopping for Mom.

Are we there yet?

Don't ask! Calculate for yourself how much longer it will take to get there on your next vacation.

1. How many miles is it to Sunshine City?

2. How fast are you going?
(Assume the driver is going the speed limit.)

3. Divide the distance by the speed to find out
how long it should take to reach your destination.

You plan to stop somewhere for lunch. About
how long will it take to get to Sandy Beach?

Hint: **For a "tenth" or "hundredth" of an hour (for example, if your answer**
is 3.25), multiply by 60 to figure out how many minutes.
.25 x 60 = 15 minutes
3.25 = 3 hours and 15 minutes

Answer:
300/65 = 4.62 hours
.62 x 60 = 37 minutes
So, it should take 4 hours and 37 minutes
to get to Sunshine City.
It will take about 1 hour and 5 minutes to
get to Sandy Beach for lunch.

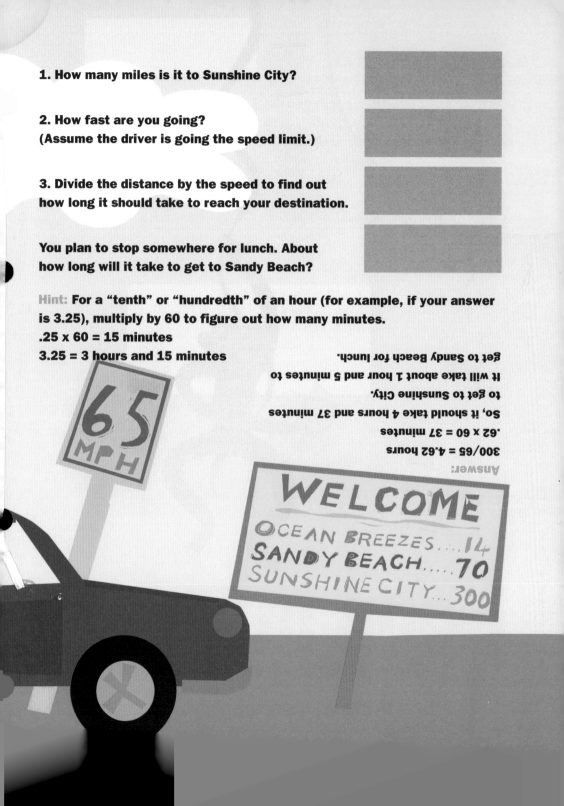

WELCOME
OCEAN BREEZES.... 14
SANDY BEACH..... 70
SUNSHINE CITY... 300

65 MPH

Hang In There!

Ask for help when you need it.

Practice your math facts.

Don't ever, EVER give up!